Dan biggar

DAN BIGGAR :

Triumph, trials and text matches

Alfred C. Wise

Dan biggar

All right reserved.No part of this publication may be reproduced, distributed,or transmitted in any form or by any means, including photocopying, recording,or other electronic mechanical methods, without the prior written permission of the publisher, except in the case of brief quotation embodied in critical reviews and certain other noncommercial uses permitted by copyright law.

Copyright © Karen lee,2023.

Dan biggar

Table of contents

INTRODUCTION

CHAPTER 1: DAN BIGGAR'S BIO

    1.1 Dan Biggar's early years

    1.2 Adoration for the game

CHAPTER 2: RISING THROUGH THE RANKS

    2.1 Initial Growth

    2.2 Entering the Professional Rugby Scene

    2.3 Becoming Associated with Wales

    2.4 Getting Past Obstacles

    2.5 Experience and Leadership

    2.6 The Rising Legacy

    2.7 Accomplishments and Significant Events

    2.8 Switch to the Saints of Northampton

    2.9 Legacy and Ongoing Development

Dan biggar

CHAPTER 3: JOINING THE OSPREYS

    3.1 Initial Relationships

    3.2 Acquiring an Ospreys contract

    3.3 Making His First Appearance

    3.4 Progress and Development

    3.5 Important Contributions

    3.6 The Ospreys' Legacy

    3.7 Dan Biggar: His Initial Flavor of Stardom

    3.8 Introducing the Ospreys to the World

    3.9 Global Acknowledgment

    3.10 The World Cup of Rugby in 2015

    3.11 Taking on a Model Role

    3.12 His Early Notoriety's Legacy

CHAPTER 4: BECOMING A KEY PLAYMAKER

    4.1 Playmaking Foundations

    4.2 Becoming an Osprey

    4.3 Global Success

    4.4 Influence and Leadership

Dan biggar

    4.5 Game Management and Tactical Awareness

    4.6 Legacy as a Crucial Actor

CHAPTER 5: INTERNATIONAL DEBUT FOR WALES

    5.1 How to Get Selected Internationally

    5.2 The First Meeting

    5.3 Highlights of the Performance

    5.4 The Debut's Impact

    5.5 The Debut's Legacy

CHAPTER 6: LEADING WALES IN SIX NATIONS GLORY

    6.1 The Six Nations Tournament

    6.2 The Grand Slam of the 2012 Six Nations

    6.3 Six Nations Championship for 2019

    6.4 Field Leadership

    6.5 Success Legacy

CHAPTER 7 : RUGBY WORLD CUP 2019

    7.1 Pre Tournament Expectations

Dan biggar

    7.2 Performance on the Pool Stage

    7.3 Wales vs. France quarter final

    7.4 Wales vs. South Africa semi final

    7.5 The 2019 World Cup's Legacy

CHAPTER 8: GOING TO NORTHAMPTON SAINTS

    8.1 Justifications for the Change

    8.2 Reaching the Saints of Northampton

    8.3 Effect on the Group

    8.4 Outstanding Performances

    8.5 Developing the Role

    8.6 Difficulties Encountered

    8.7 The Northampton Saints' Legacy

CHAPTER 9: MENTORSHIP AND TEAM LEADERSHIP

    9.1 The Value of Mentoring

    9.2 The Role of Team Leadership

    9.3 Creating Leaders of Tomorrow

    9.4 Long-Term Effects

Dan biggar

CHAPTER 10: BRITISH AND IRISH LIONS EXPERIENCE

    10.1 Being included in the Lions squad

    10.2 The South Africa Tour in 2021

    10.3 The Experience's Effect

    10.4 The Lions' Legacy Experience

CHAPTER 11: THE BIGGAR KICK ART AND PRECISION

    11.1 Biggar's Kicking Technical Aspects

    11.2 Understanding Tactical Situations

    11.3 Mental Sturdiness

    11.4 Effect on the Game

CHAPTER 12: OFF THE FIELD LIFE FAMILY AND BALANCE

    12.1 Domestic Life

    12.2 Individual Passions

    12.3 Handling Rugby Obligations

    12.4 Priorities for the Family

CHAPTER 13: SETBACKS AND COMEBACKS

Dan biggar

    13.1 Failures

    13.2 Returns

CHAPTER 14: THE BIGGAR'S LEGACY AND THE NEXT GENERATION

    14.1 The Legacy of Biggar

    14.2 Impact on the Upcoming Generation

    14.3 Prospects for the Future

CHAPTER 15: LOOKING FORWARD BEYOND THE PITCH

    15.1 Mentoring and Coaching

    15.2 Analysis and Punditry

    15.3 Supporting the Welfare of Players

    15.4 Ambassadorship for Rugby

    15.5 Volunteering and Community Service

    15.6 Entrepreneurship

CHAPTER 16: REFLECTION FROM A RUGBY LEGEND

    16.1 Taking Pride in Wales' Representation

    16.2 Characteristics

Dan biggar

16.3 Leadership Lessons Learned

16.4 Appreciation of Mentors and Supporters

16.5 Establishing a Heritage

16.6 Toward the Future

CONCLUSION

Dan biggar

INTRODUCTION

Dan Biggar is one of the most devoted, strategic, and uncompromising rugby players in the game. Biggar has made a lasting impression on Welsh rugby and international competition thanks to his accuracy, intense competitive spirit, and unwavering dedication on the field. Dan Biggar: Triumphs, Trials, and Test Matches explores the significant events, crucial games, and personal struggles that have influenced this outstanding fly-half's life and career.

Biggar's tale is one of perseverance and determination, from his early Swansea days to his rise to prominence in the Welsh national squad. In addition to his notorious

Dan biggar

Biggarena ritual and strong kicks, fans admire him for his capacity to lead under duress.

Dan biggar

CHAPTER 1: DAN BIGGAR'S BIO

Dan Biggar is renowned for his talent, leadership, and accuracy on the field. Biggar, who was born in Morriston, Swansea, on October 16, 1989, plays as a fly-half, a position essential to controlling the game's strategy, creating plays, and frequently acting as the primary kicker. He is a notable player in Welsh rugby because of his strong kicking, careful planning, and enthusiastic performance.

With the Ospreys, a Welsh regional club, Biggar started his professional career. He immediately established himself as a star due to his remarkable kicking accuracy

Dan biggar

and passion for competition. After he joined the Welsh national team and made his debut in 2008, his reputation grew. Since then, he has emerged as a pivotal player in Wales's Six Nations campaigns, guiding the squad to multiple titles and Grand Slams with standout performances that have won him admirers.

Apart from his achievements with Wales, Biggar has participated in high-profile Southern Hemisphere tours as a member of the British and Irish Lions, a top-tier squad made up of players from England, Ireland, Scotland, and Wales. In the English Premiership, he currently plays for the Northampton Saints, where his playmaking abilities and experience continue to have an influence.

Biggar is renowned for his fierce on-field personality and competitive spirit, which are especially evident in

Dan biggar his well-known pre-kick performance, known as the Biggarena. He is one of rugby's most admired fly-halves because of his methodical style, keen tactical awareness, and capacity for high-pressure play. He is respected as a mentor and role model off the field, inspiring the upcoming generation of players in Wales and elsewhere.

1.1 Dan Biggar's early years

On October 16, 1989, Dan Biggar was born in Morriston, Swansea, a town rich in rugby culture and history. Rugby was a part of Dan's upbringing in a tiny Welsh town, and he soon developed a fondness for it. Early on, he picked up a rugby ball and began playing with neighborhood teams, displaying remarkable aptitude and tenacity right away.

Dan biggar

Biggar's parents supported his early participation in the sport since they saw his passion and innate talent. He joined the local rugby team Gorseinon RFC, where he immediately made a name for himself as a competitive player with a great work ethic and a talent for creating plays. He possessed a strong focus and a desire to get better even as a young player, traits that would later define his professional career.

Dan's talent was cultivated during his adolescent years at Gowerton Comprehensive School, which boasted a robust rugby program. He kept improving his abilities and knowledge of the game, particularly the nuances of the fly-half position. His remarkable kicking accuracy, tactical knowledge, and leadership abilities distinguished him as one of Welsh rugby's most promising young players by the time he was in his late teens.

Dan biggar

Biggar's early years were characterized by a strong competitive edge in addition to his developing abilities. On the training field, he was renowned for his determination, frequently lingering beyond practices to improve his kicking technique, which would later prove to be a key factor in his success. His development was not overlooked, and he soon attracted the interest of local teams, which ultimately resulted in his hiring by the Ospreys, one of Wales's best professional rugby teams.

These early years shaped Biggar into the tough, disciplined, and fearless player that supporters would grow to respect, laying the groundwork for his rugby career. The principles he was taught in his early years—dedication, pride in playing for Wales, and a never-ending quest for progress—would help him navigate the difficulties of his professional career and solidify his status as one of Wales' most significant rugby players.

Dan biggar

1.2 Adoration for the game

From his unwavering passion on the field to his disciplined attitude, Dan Biggar's love for rugby is apparent in every facet of his game. He was enthralled with rugby from a young age, drawn to its intensity, camaraderie, and the sense of pride it gave to players and supporters, having grown up in a rugby-loving area of Wales. His passion and respect for the game were the only things that could equal his innate brilliance, and they would come to define his career.

Biggar's dedication extends beyond his playing; he has a profound respect for every aspect of the game. He is renowned for his meticulous preparation, devoting additional hours to honing his kicks, watching game

Dan biggar

tapes, and coming up with fresh ideas to improve his performance. His distinctive kicking technique, known as the Biggarena, is more than simply a peculiarity; it's evidence of his commitment to his art and shows how seriously he takes each play. His dedication to every facet of the game is demonstrated by this routine and his capacity to perform under duress.

His pride in representing Wales is another indication of his passion for rugby. Biggar believes that donning the Welsh shirt is about more than just his accomplishments; it's about capturing the essence of Welsh rugby, paying tribute to his predecessors, and motivating future generations. Biggar often cites playing for Wales in front of fervent Welsh supporters as the highlight of his career when questioned about his most memorable moments.

Sharing the game with younger generations is another aspect of Biggar's enthusiasm. He is renowned for

Dan biggar coaching up-and-coming athletes, helping them to cultivate not only their abilities but also a sincere appreciation for the game. His passion for rugby extends beyond his perseverance; it also aims to build a resilient, respectful, and dedicated rugby community.

Essentially, every punt, every tackle, and every second Dan Biggar spends on the field reflects his passion for rugby. He has endured the highs and lows of his career because of this enduring dedication, which has solidified his reputation as one of rugby's most devoted and inspirational leaders.

Dan biggar

CHAPTER 2: RISING THROUGH THE RANKS

Dan Biggar's ascent through the rugby ranks is evidence of his skill, tenacity, and uncompromising work ethic. His journey from a young, talented player in local clubs to an international standout exemplifies the tenacity and commitment that characterize the ideal rugby career.

2.1 Initial Growth

Dan biggar

At an early age, Biggar started playing rugby with Swansea's Gorseinon RFC. He immediately established himself as a proficient fly-half after showcasing his potential at a young age. He stood out from his colleagues due to his remarkable kicking skills, strategic thinking, and intense competitiveness. Biggar was able to refine his abilities and obtain invaluable on-field experience through his early participation in juvenile rugby.

2.2 Entering the Professional Rugby Scene

Biggar became the youngest player to gain 100 caps for the area when he made his Ospreys debut at the age of 18. Strong game management, poise beyond his years, and a talent for grabbing crucial moments characterized his club match performances. But it took him some time

Dan biggar

to earn a berth on the national squad. To test his ability to withstand the demands of international rugby, he had to battle against seasoned fly-halves.

2.3 Becoming Associated with Wales

Following a string of sporadic appearances, Biggar made his breakthrough and cemented his position as a starting fly-half during the 2013 Six Nations Championship. His consistent play, which demonstrated his development and preparedness for the big stage, helped Wales win the tournament. He went on to establish himself as a vital member of Wales, renowned for his unwavering work ethic, clever kicking, and ferocious tackling.

Dan biggar

2.4 Getting Past Obstacles

Biggar experienced many setbacks during his career, such as injuries and criticism of his style of play. But he turned these setbacks into motivation to sharpen his skills and bounce back stronger. He gained the respect of both opponents and teammates for his perseverance in the face of hardship and dedication to constant growth.

2.5 Experience and Leadership

Biggar developed as a leader on the field over time. He became a trusted member of the Welsh team due to his experience and wisdom, which led to his selection as captain for the 2022 Six Nations. As a captain, he exemplified the traits of a leader who advanced through

Dan biggar the ranks with hard work and merit, leading with enthusiasm and setting a high bar for those around him.

2.6 The Rising Legacy

Young players are inspired by Biggar's journey from club rugby to playing a key role in Wales' most significant triumphs. His story serves as a reminder that hard effort, perseverance, and an unwavering will to keep going are just as important to success as skill.

Dan biggar

2.7 Accomplishments and Significant Events

Biggar's rise through the rugby ranks is highlighted by the many milestones he has accomplished throughout his career. He has participated in several Six Nations competitions and helped Wales win the Grand Slam. His status as one of the best fly-halves in the game was further cemented in 2017 when he was selected for the British and Irish Lions.

2.8 Switch to the Saints of Northampton

Biggar advanced in his career in 2020 when he joined the English Premiership's Northampton Saints. By making this change, he was able to apply his extensive knowledge in a new setting and increase his impact in

Dan biggar

rugby. As he adjusted to the demands of a new league, his leadership and playmaking skills were evident.

2.9 Legacy and Ongoing Development

The narrative of Dan Biggar's ascent through the ranks is one of perseverance, hard effort, and an everlasting love for rugby. He has emerged as a figurehead for aspiring gamers, proving that commitment, constant development, and a passion for the game are the keys to success. Biggar's path serves as an inspiration as he continues to compete at the top levels, demonstrating that anyone can achieve greatness in rugby with hard work and dedication.

Dan biggar

CHAPTER 3: JOINING THE OSPREYS

A significant turning point in Dan Biggar's rugby career, his journey to join the Ospreys showcases his commitment and developing skill. The Ospreys, one of Wales' top professional rugby teams, took notice of him when he showed remarkable promise at school and local clubs.

3.1 Initial Relationships

Biggar was developing his abilities and laying a strong foundation as a fly-half in the youth divisions over the years preceding his signing. His exploits with Swansea

Dan biggar

Schools and Gorseinon RFC demonstrated his innate skill, powerful kicking game, and tactical knowledge. His eventual move to professional rugby was made possible by regional selectors who saw his potential and started closely monitoring him.

3.2 Acquiring an Ospreys contract

Biggar joined the Ospreys in 2008 at the age of 18. He was entering a professional setting with seasoned players and established talent, thus this transfer was important for the team as well as for hly. He was able to train with some of the top players in the game and compete at the highest level after joining the Ospreys.

3.3 Making His First Appearance

Dan biggar

Biggar demonstrated his abilities in the Celtic League when he made his professional debut for the Ospreys in 2008. Despite his youth and the intense competition for the fly-half position, he soon showed his maturity and confidence on the field. He had an instant influence and gained the respect of both coaches and teammates for his powerful kicking and game management.

3.4 Progress and Development

Biggar encountered the mental and physical strains of playing at a high level as well as other difficulties associated with professional rugby as he adapted to the Ospreys setup. He constantly pushed himself to get better by working hard on his technical abilities, tactical awareness, and physical fitness. He started to get more playing time and establish himself as a vital member of the team as a result of his hard work.

Dan biggar

Biggar played with several of the Ospreys' top players in his early years, picking up tips from their experiences and developing a deeper understanding of the professional game. He rose through the ranks swiftly thanks to his work ethic and eagerness to learn, and he is now regarded as one of Welsh rugby's most potential fly-halves.

3.5 Important Contributions

During his tenure with the Ospreys, Biggar made significant contributions to the team. He gained notoriety for his ability to direct attacking plays, manage the game's tempo, and make clutch kicks when things became tight. He played a key role in the Ospreys' notable triumphs in the Pro12 (now the United Rugby Championship) and European tournaments.

Dan biggar

Biggar's leadership skills also started to emerge as he became a dependable playmaker. On the field, he showed that he could motivate his teammates by offering support and direction. His role as a key member of the Ospreys team was cemented by his remarkable skill set and developing leadership.

3.6 The Ospreys' Legacy

Both individual and team success characterized Biggar's tenure with the Ospreys, and his fervent performances and dedication to the team made him a fan favorite. During a pivotal time in Welsh rugby history, he helped the Ospreys win important games and helped the squad develop.

Dan biggar

All things considered, Dan Biggar's career was completely changed by joining the Ospreys, which helped him hone his abilities, acquire priceless experience, and set the stage for his future triumphs with the team and the Welsh national team. He became the outstanding player he is today thanks in part to his time with the Ospreys, and his legacy will continue to motivate rugby players in Wales for years to come.

3.7 Dan Biggar: His Initial Flavor of Stardom

A string of crucial events marked the beginning of Dan Biggar's rugby career, showcasing his skill, diligence, and willpower. The success of the clubs he played for, especially in his early years with the Ospreys and the Welsh national team, gave him his first taste of stardom in addition to his accomplishments.

Dan biggar

3.8 Introducing the Ospreys to the World

When Biggar joined the Ospreys in 2008, his career took off. His outstanding kicking skills, game intelligence, and leadership traits were all on display in his impressive performances throughout his first campaign. Around this time, he began to become well-known outside of his local club. His first notable breakthrough occurred during the 2010–2011 season when he was instrumental in the Ospreys' Pro12 triumph and helped the team win the championship.

Biggar swiftly established himself as an important member of the Ospreys' squad thanks to his outstanding performances, which included several pivotal kicks and strategic plays. As the youthful fly-half demonstrated his capacity to play well under duress, the media started to take notice of him and his reputation increased. His rise

Dan biggar to prominence was sparked by his deft play, perseverance, and love for the game.

3.9 Global Acknowledgment

When Biggar, then just 19 years old, made his debut for the Welsh national team in 2008, his fame skyrocketed. His first outings allowed him to test his abilities against some of the world's top players and compete on an international level. His destiny as a national celebrity was established by this exposure, which also raised his profile.

The 2012 Six Nations Championship was one of the pivotal events in Biggar's early international career. He was instrumental in Wales' Grand Slam victory, which won over supporters and cemented his place as a vital member of the national team. His debut on the

Dan biggar international scene and the tournament's high point came from his performance against England, in which he effectively kicked a vital penalty.

3.10 The World Cup of Rugby in 2015

As a notable player for Wales at the 2015 Rugby World Cup, Dan Biggar experienced his first taste of real celebrity. He had a great opportunity to demonstrate his abilities to a worldwide audience at the competition. Wales advanced to the knockout stages because of his excellent kicking accuracy, tactical understanding, and poise under duress.

Fans, pundits, and past players all praised Biggar for his performances during the tournament. His reputation as one of the world's top fly-halves was cemented by his

Dan biggar ability to perform crucial plays and step up under duress. In addition to growing his fan base, the publicity he received at the World Cup cemented his place as a rugby household figure.

3.11 Taking on a Model Role

Dan Biggar started to realize the responsibility that came with being a well-known person in the sport as his celebrity grew. For new athletes hoping to follow in his footsteps, he became an inspiration. Fans and young rugby fans alike were moved by Biggar's hard ethic, humility, and commitment to the game. He frequently talked about how proud he was to wear the national jersey and how important it was to represent Wales.

He was able to take advantage of chances outside of the field because of his increased reputation. Biggar used his

Dan biggar position to improve the community by being involved in several humanitarian endeavors. Fans were further won over by his dedication to giving back, which also demonstrated the kind of person he was off the field.

3.12 His Early Notoriety's Legacy

Dan Biggar began a great career that would see him continue to ascend in the sport with his first taste of recognition. His time with the Ospreys and the Welsh national team prepared him for success in the future and paved the way for his rise to prominence as one of rugby's best fly-halves.

In the end, Biggar's early notoriety was shaped by both his on-field accomplishments and his demeanor as a player and a person. In addition to inspiring innumerable

Dan biggar supporters and aspiring athletes, his devotion to the game, devotion to his team, and drive to change the world have permanently altered Welsh rugby.

Dan biggar

CHAPTER 4: BECOMING A KEY PLAYMAKER

The tale of Dan Biggar's transformation into a crucial rugby playmaker is one of leadership, skill development, and tactical awareness. Biggar's journey from his early days in small clubs to his rise to prominence as a key member of the Ospreys and the Welsh national team is marked by his profound knowledge of the game, superb decision-making skills, and capacity to perform well under duress.

4.1 Playmaking Foundations

Dan biggar

When Biggar was younger, he immediately made a name for himself as a gifted fly-half. He gained a wide range of skills while playing for Swansea Schools and Gorseinon RFC, including accurate kicking, tactical awareness, and game reading. His early experiences prepared him for his future as a crucial playmaker by assisting him in understanding the subtleties of the fly-half position.

4.2 Becoming an Osprey

Biggar was entering a professional setting where he would refine his playmaking skills when he joined the Ospreys in 2008. He faced more seasoned players in his first season, and although it was a learning curve, he seized the chance. Biggar's innate leadership abilities started to show as he swiftly adjusted to the fast-paced environment of professional rugby.

Dan biggar

Biggar accepted the responsibility of being a fly-half while he was with the Ospreys. He developed his ability to lead assaults, control games, and make snap judgments that may decide a match. He immediately established a reputation for accuracy and poise, and his superb kicking skills, both from hand and at goal, made him a dependable choice in stressful circumstances.

Biggar accepted the responsibility of being a fly-half while he was with the Ospreys. He developed his ability to lead assaults, control games, and make snap judgments that may decide a match. He immediately established a reputation for accuracy and poise, and his superb kicking skills, both from hand and at goal, made him a dependable choice in stressful circumstances.

He became a key component of the Ospreys' strategy because of his ability to take the initiative and make big

Dan biggar plays. His on-field acumen, which enabled him to predict the opposition's actions and take advantage of holes in their defense, was acknowledged by coaches and teammates.

4.3 Global Success

Biggar's steady selection for the Welsh national team was the pinnacle of his rise to prominence as a crucial playmaker. His 2008 debut was only the start of his international career; he made an impression at the 2012 Six Nations Championship. Biggar became an essential part of Wales' plan as they looked to regain their place among rugby's top teams.

Dan biggar

His efforts throughout the 2012 Six Nations in particular demonstrated his capacity to direct play and guide the team in crucial situations. By planning assaults and delivering clutch kicks that sealed important points, he played a key role in Wales' Grand Slam triumph. His reputation as one of the best fly halves in the game was solidified by his ability to play at the highest level and his tactical acumen.

4.4 Influence and Leadership

Biggar's leadership abilities were more apparent as he developed as a player. He exuded a combination of confidence and humility, which naturally earned him the respect of his teammates. Biggar's status as a crucial playmaker was further cemented by his readiness to assume accountability in stressful situations.

Dan biggar

Beyond his performances, he became a mentor to the team's younger players, giving them advice on how to approach the game strategically. Biggar's knowledge and perspectives were crucial in assisting the next Welsh players in comprehending the intricacies of playmaking.

4.5 Game Management and Tactical Awareness

Biggar's tactical awareness and game management are two characteristics that set him apart as a player. He has an excellent sense of timing; depending on the circumstance, he knows when to slow down or speed up the game. He can make tactical choices that alter the outcome of a match because of his ability to analyze the opposition's defense and predict their moves.

Dan biggar

Biggar's kicking technique is really impressive. His versatility as a playmaker is demonstrated by his accuracy from the tee and his ability to execute tactical kicks for offensive or territorial opportunities. He has regularly scored important conversions and penalties, greatly assisting his squad in their scoring endeavors.

4.6 Legacy as a Crucial Actor

Dan Biggar's development as a crucial playmaker is evidence of his commitment, aptitude, and rugby knowledge. He is a notable personality in the sport because of his capacity to manage games, make clutch plays, and guide his team under duress. His legacy as a crucial playmaker is well-established as he continues to play at the top levels for the Ospreys and the Welsh

Dan biggar national team, encouraging upcoming players to take on the duties and responsibilities of the fly-half position.

Dan biggar

CHAPTER 5: INTERNATIONAL DEBUT FOR WALES

An important turning point in Dan Biggar's rugby career was his debut for Wales, which paved the way for his rise to prominence as one of the world's best fly-halves. His path to this crucial point was marked by commitment, diligence, and an unwavering quest for sporting greatness.

5.1 How to Get Selected Internationally

Biggar was chosen to play for Wales internationally after showcasing remarkable skill with the Ospreys and

Dan biggar winning accolades in domestic events. He is a strong contender for national selection because of his performances in the Pro12 and European competitions, which demonstrated his skill set, including his tactical awareness, kicking precision, and game management abilities.

In 2008, at the age of 19, he received his first call-up to the Welsh team. Even though he was young, his skill and confidence got him a position in the starting lineup for a game against the Barbarians, a classic matchup that frequently combines well-known players with up-and-coming talent. This would be his first time donning the recognizable red jersey.

5.2 The First Meeting

Dan biggar

In a friendly encounter against the Barbarians at Cardiff's Millennium Stadium on June 30, 2008, Dan Biggar made his Wales debut. In addition to being important for Biggar individually, this game gave the Welsh squad a chance to try out new players and tactics.

Biggar, playing for his nation on the international scene for the first time, came into the game feeling both nervous and excited. Even though it was an exhibition game, the atmosphere was electrifying, with fervent Welsh supporters supporting their team.

5.3 Highlights of the Performance

Biggar showed hints of the abilities that would later characterize his career on his debut. He displayed his innate talent, poise, and ability to read the game despite his youth and relative inexperience. Even as he dealt with the difficulties of playing with more seasoned international players, his tactical kicking and decision-making talents benefited the squad in pivotal situations.

Biggar's performance was encouraging and set the stage for his future choices, even though Wales lost the game. The teenage fly-half gained crucial experience playing at the international level, which gave him a better understanding of the pressures and rigors of playing rugby internationally.

5.4 The Debut's Impact

The beginning of Biggar's lengthy and remarkable international career was his debut. After making his debut, he steadily established himself as a vital member of the Welsh team and continued to be selected. His

Dan biggar latter performances demonstrated his improvement as a fly-half, including pivotal games in the Six Nations and World Cups.

Biggar would go on to accomplish important milestones throughout the years, including leading Wales to a Grand Slam win in 2012 and performing admirably in the 2015 Rugby World Cup. His rise from rookie to senior member of the national team is a testament to his skill as well as his dedication to the game and hard work.

5.5 The Debut's Legacy

More than just a personal accomplishment, Dan Biggar's international debut marked the start of an incredible journey that would make him one of the most influential players in Welsh rugby. He would go on to win praise,

Dan biggar

admiration, and a reputation as one of the sport's most dependable fly-halves for his later exploits for Wales.

Biggar's debut is still seen as a turning point in his career, a testament to his progress and the commitment needed to compete at the top levels of rugby. His debut stands as a tribute to the value of tenacity and enthusiasm in the pursuit of sporting achievement, as he continues to represent Wales on the international scene.

Dan biggar

CHAPTER 6: LEADING WALES IN SIX NATIONS GLORY

Dan Biggar's status as one of the best fly-halves in international rugby has been cemented by his contribution to Wales' Six Nations Championship triumph. Wales won several Six Nations championships with his leadership, skill, and poise under duress, especially during their Grand Slam campaigns.

6.1 The Six Nations Tournament

Dan biggar

The national teams of England, France, Ireland, Italy, Scotland, and Wales compete in the Six Nations Championship, one of rugby's most prominent competitions. It takes not just individual skill but also unified teamwork and smart execution to compete against such strong opponents. Biggar was a tremendous help to the Welsh team because of his knowledge of the game and his ability to control the flow of play.

6.2 The Grand Slam of the 2012 Six Nations

Biggar's international career took a dramatic turn in 2012 when he made important contributions during the Six Nations Championship. Despite not being the starting fly-half at the start of the competition, he was given the chance to play important roles when the squad was affected by injuries. His excellent kicking and strategic game management helped Wales win a hard-fought

Dan biggar match against England, making his performance especially remarkable.

Biggar had a bigger impact on the team's offensive plan as the competition went on. Wales was able to win difficult games against strong opponents thanks to his ability to control the game's pace and make wise choices under duress. Biggar demonstrated his patience and composure in a high-stakes situation during the last match against France, which was essential in winning the Grand Slam.

6.3 Six Nations Championship for 2019

Biggar was crucial to Wales' success in the 2019 Six Nations Championship, showcasing his leadership and talent once again. Biggar was one of the main players on a team led by head coach Warren Gatland that sought to win the championship again. He was able to offer

Dan biggar stability in the fly-half position thanks to his knowledge of the game and experience, which was crucial for team cohesiveness and game plan execution.

Biggar's ability to kick for points and tactical territory was a notable aspect of the event. He frequently converted tries and executed important penalties, demonstrating his dependability as a kicker under duress. In addition to helping Wales acquire important territory, his tactical kicking gave his teammates attacking opportunities.

Biggar's performance against England in the last round, where his tactical choices and game management were crucial to Wales' triumph, was one of the tournament's high points. His confidence was evident in high-pressure circumstances, and he demonstrated an improving ability to lead the team both on and off the field.

Dan biggar

6.4 Field Leadership

Biggar's leadership is essential as a fly-half. During games, he is frequently the player in charge of calling plays, sharing strategy, and making snap judgments. His poise and self-assurance motivate his teammates, giving the team faith and resolve.

Biggar showed both technical skill and emotional intelligence during his Six Nations campaigns, recognizing the game's dynamics and modifying his strategy accordingly. His ability to lead proved especially crucial during stressful situations, as his composed manner served to keep the team under control.

Dan biggar

6.5 Success Legacy

The history of Wales has been profoundly impacted by Dan Biggar's efforts to the team's Six Nations triumph. In addition to receiving praise, his exploits during important competitions, such as the Grand Slam campaigns, have made him a national hero in Wales. His capacity to lead from the front and perform well under duress has established a benchmark for rugby players in the future.

Biggar's legacy as a Six Nations leader is still important as he plays rugby at the top levels of the international game. He is an example to prospective players hoping to establish themselves in the sport because he exemplifies the tenacity, grit, and enthusiasm that characterize Welsh rugby.

Dan biggar

CHAPTER 7 : RUGBY WORLD CUP 2019

For Dan Biggar and the Welsh national side, the 2019 Rugby World Cup in Japan was a crucial competition that demonstrated both individual skill and teamwork on a global scale. Biggar, one of rugby's top fly-halves, was instrumental in taking Wales to the semifinals and made a substantial contribution to the team's overall success during the competition.

7.1 Pre Tournament Expectations

Before the World Cup, Wales entered the tournament as one of the favorites, having enjoyed a successful run in the Six Nations and established a solid squad under head

Dan biggar
coach Warren Gatland. Dan Biggar, known for his tactical kicking, game management, and leadership skills, was a key figure in the team's strategy. With expectations high, Biggar was determined to leave his mark on the tournament and help Wales achieve their goal of securing a World Cup title.

7.2 Performance on the Pool Stage

Wales, Australia, Fiji, Georgia, and Uruguay were all assigned to Pool D. As the team advanced through the pool rounds and won all four games, Biggar's expertise and talent were clear to see.

1. Wales vs. Georgia: Biggar contributed points with penalties and conversions in Wales' first game against Georgia, showcasing his kicking accuracy. Wales won

Dan biggar

43–14 thanks in large part to his ability to dominate the game from fly-half.

2. Australia vs. Wales: The much-awaited matchup with Australia was a pivotal point in the pool stage. Biggar played a key role in this game by kicking strategically and managing the game well. Wales won 29–25 thanks in part to his smart kicks that helped them gain territory and his calm kicking under duress that allowed him to convert penalties. This triumph was noteworthy because it demonstrated Wales' tenacity and strategic skill against a strong foe.

3. Wales vs. Fiji: Biggar showed off his playmaking skills while maintaining his strong performance against Fiji. Wales won 29–17 thanks in large part to his assault planning and execution. Biggar's leadership on the field was strengthened by his ability to read the game and generate opportunities for his teammates.

Dan biggar

4. Biggar was instrumental in helping Wales defeat Uruguay 35–13 in the last pool encounter, guaranteeing they won their group and went to the knockout stages.

7.3 Wales vs. France quarter final

Wales and France had a tense and fiercely fought match in the quarterfinals. Biggar's strategic kicking and experience were essential in helping Wales win by a slim margin of 20–19.

Biggar's ability to remain composed under duress enabled him to keep control of the game and make crucial choices that directed his team's offensive strategy. He contributed to important plays that kept the

Dan biggar scoreboard moving and gave Wales vital points. His performance demonstrated his capacity to motivate and guide his teammates in stressful situations.

7.4 Wales vs. South Africa semi final

South Africa presented Wales with a formidable task in the semifinals. Both sides were fighting for a spot in the final, and the encounter was characterized by fierce physicality and tactical skirmishes. Biggar's leadership and tenacity were evident as he handled the intricacies of the game.

Biggar's performance was praiseworthy, even if Wales lost 19–16 in the end. He played a key role in planning the assault by making important choices under duress. Wales remained competitive throughout the game thanks

Dan biggar

to his kicking and game management, demonstrating his capacity to play at his best under trying conditions.

7.5 The 2019 World Cup's Legacy

Dan Biggar's position as one of the best fly-halves in international rugby was cemented at the 2019 Rugby World Cup, which was a turning point in his career. His performances during the competition showed off not only his technical proficiency but also his capacity for leadership and fortitude under duress.

Wales' run to the semifinals demonstrated the team's strength and the influence of stars like Biggar, even though they were unable to make it to the final. His superb play and capacity to motivate and guide his teammates have a lasting impact on Welsh rugby.

As Biggar's career progresses, the 2019 World Cup will be viewed as evidence of his skill and commitment to the

Dan biggar game, acting as a springboard for more accomplishments on the global scene.

Dan biggar

CHAPTER 8: GOING TO NORTHAMPTON SAINTS

A new chapter in Dan Biggar's remarkable rugby career began in 2020 when he joined the Northampton Saints, giving him the chance to take on new challenges and advance as a premier fly-half. Biggar's move from Welsh rugby to the English Premiership was important for him on a personal and professional level since it gave him the chance to improve his abilities and contribute to a competitive club atmosphere.

8.1 Justifications for the Change

Dan biggar

Biggar thought it was time for a change of pace after a successful stint with the Ospreys, where he became a household figure in Welsh rugby. His choice to join Northampton Saints was mostly influenced by his desire to play at the greatest level and investigate new prospects in a different division. Along with contributing his extensive knowledge to a new squad, the transfer gave him the chance to see England's thriving rugby culture.

8.2 Reaching the Saints of Northampton

Biggar was greeted by the Saints as a high-profile addition and a vital member who would impact the squad on and off the field. He was a great asset to the team because of his reputation as a talented fly-half who was renowned for his leadership, tactical kicking, and game management. Biggar's professionalism and

Dan biggar expertise were considered essential for mentoring the team's younger players during the Saints' rebuilding phase.

Biggar assimilated into the team right away and developed close bonds with the coaching staff and teammates. His commitment to training and work ethic complemented the club's ethos, which made it easier for him to fit in.

8.3 Effect on the Group

Biggar demonstrated his extraordinary skill set in his debut games, making a substantial contribution to the Saints' offensive tactics. He was able to efficiently direct play and carry out tactical kicks because of his ability to understand the game and make snap choices. Biggar's

Dan biggar international rugby background also gave the team insightful advice, particularly for younger players who needed direction under pressure.

As he assumed a mentoring role and contributed to the development of Northampton's next generation of talent, his leadership abilities were put on display. His presence on the training field and in the locker room gave his teammates confidence and fostered a supportive team atmosphere.

8.4 Outstanding Performances

Biggar had several memorable games in his first season with the Northampton Saints. He frequently contributed significantly to winning games because of his precise kicking and tactical knowledge.

Dan biggar

1. Crucial Games: Biggar's impact was most noticeable during crucial games, as his tactical leadership enabled the Saints to win close games. His reputation as a consistent match-winner was demonstrated by his ability to perform clutch kicks under duress.

2. European Competitions: Biggar was able to further shine by participating in European events. His ability to adjust to various playing styles while upholding his high standards was demonstrated by his efforts in the European Rugby Champions Cup. Playing against elite European clubs presented hurdles that he overcame because of his international rugby expertise.

8.5 Developing the Role

Dan biggar

Biggar became more at ease in his position with Northampton as the season went on. He formed close bonds with other important members of the team, which improved the group's performance as a whole. He was able to lead the backline and create scoring opportunities because he comprehended the game and his ability to communicate with teammates.

In addition to improving his performance, his move to the Northampton Saints aided in the team's general expansion and improvement. Biggar demonstrated his leadership both on and off the field, and he became a pivotal player in the Saints' comeback.

8.6 Difficulties Encountered

Dan biggar

Biggar encountered difficulties adjusting to a new club environment and a different style of play, even though the transfer was generally good. It took time and effort to get used to the English Premiership's dynamics and establish a rapport with new teammates. However, he was able to overcome these obstacles thanks to his professionalism and dedication to the team.

8.7 The Northampton Saints' Legacy

A major turning point in Dan Biggar's career was his transfer to the Northampton Saints, which allowed him to continue competing at the highest level while expanding his horizons. He immediately made a significant contribution to the team by becoming a vital leader and playmaker.

Dan biggar

Biggar's legacy with the Saints will be determined by his talent, leadership, and capacity to motivate others as he continues to contribute to the team's success. His tenure with the Northampton Saints further cemented his status as one of rugby's top players and is evidence of his versatility and commitment to the game.

Dan biggar

CHAPTER 9: MENTORSHIP AND TEAM LEADERSHIP

In addition to showcasing his outstanding playing skills, Dan Biggar's move to the Northampton Saints also brought attention to his leadership and mentoring role within the club. His prior club success and international rugby experience made him a valuable leader who could mentor younger players and shape the team's .

9.1 The Value of Mentoring

In professional sports, mentoring is essential, particularly in a fast-paced, cutthroat setting like rugby. Biggar, a seasoned player, understood the need to impart his wisdom and experiences to younger players to assist

Dan biggar
them improve their abilities and self-assurance on the field. His mentoring methodology comprised

1. Setting an Example Younger players looked up to Biggar's discipline, work ethic, and dedication to training. His commitment to raising his own game encouraged others to follow suit, thereby reaffirming the team's core ideals of diligence and tenacity.

2. Exchange of Knowledge Biggar's vast experience competing internationally allowed him to offer priceless insights into the tactical and mental facets of the game. He assisted younger players in comprehending the subtleties of making decisions, managing their games, and handling pressure in high-stakes situations.

9.2 The Role of Team Leadership

Dan biggar

Naturally, Biggar assumed a leadership role within the team as one of the more experienced players at Northampton Saints. His duties went beyond the field because he was instrumental in establishing the team's culture and encouraging camaraderie among the players.

1. Communication: During practice and games, Biggar had exceptional communication skills with his teammates. Better on-field coordination was made possible by his ability to communicate intricate tactics in a straightforward and succinct style, which kept everyone on the team in sync.

2. Game Management: Biggar's ability to control games on the field demonstrated his leadership. He oversaw play, made tactical choices, and offered direction as needed. He was able to give his teammates confidence by remaining composed under duress, which strengthened their faith in the strategy.

3. Encouraging Teammates: Biggar's zeal and love for the game inspired the whole team into action. He fostered a competitive spirit among his teammates by encouraging them to take on challenges and aim for perfection. Even in difficult circumstances, his upbeat demeanor kept spirits high and concentration high.

9.3 Creating Leaders of Tomorrow

Biggar's dedication to cultivating the team's future leaders was one of his most significant achievements as a mentor and leader. He recognized that developing young talent and allowing them to assume leadership roles were critical to the Saints' long-term success.

Dan biggar

1. Promoting Initiative During practice and games, Biggar pushed younger players to take charge, which helped them gain confidence and decision-making abilities. He fostered their leadership potential by giving them chances to lead particular exercises or conversations.

2. Promoting an Environment of Collaboration Biggar advocated for a collaborative style of leadership, stressing the value of cooperation and group accountability. To prove ownership and unity, he urged players to express their thoughts and participate in team tactics.

3. Offering Helpful Criticism In his role as a mentor, Biggar gave younger players helpful criticism so they could pinpoint their areas of weakness while also acknowledging their accomplishments. His fair-minded

Dan biggar approach to criticism encouraged the team to learn and develop continuously.

9.4 Long-Term Effects

The Northampton Saints have been impacted for a long time by Dan Biggar's team leadership and mentoring. In addition to improving the team's performance, his capacity to relate to players, set a good example, and impart his extensive expertise has fostered a growth-oriented atmosphere.

As Biggar continues his career with the Saints, his role as a mentor and leader will remain integral to the team's success. His dedication to developing future generations of rugby talent exemplifies the qualities of a true leader, ensuring that his legacy extends beyond his playing days. By investing in the growth of his teammates, Biggar is not only shaping the present success of the

Dan biggar
Saints but also laying the foundation for the club's future.

Dan biggar

CHAPTER 10: BRITISH AND IRISH LIONS EXPERIENCE

The high point of Dan Biggar's rugby career has been his participation with the British and Irish Lions, which has allowed him to play with and against some of the world's top players. Being chosen for the British and Irish Lions, a team that includes players from England, Ireland, Scotland, and Wales, is a great honor. The team goes on important tours every four years.

10.1 Being included in the Lions squad

Biggar's inclusion in the British and Irish Lions' 2021 tour to South Africa was evidence of his abilities,

Dan biggar background, and contributions to rugby internationally. He was a strong contender for selection because of his exceptional Six Nations performances and his leadership position with the Welsh national team. His position in the team was further cemented by his tactical skill as a fly-half and his capacity to perform well under duress.

10.2 The South Africa Tour in 2021

The 2021 Lions tour was special since it was held during the COVID-19 epidemic, which had an impact on logistics and travel. Three test matches against the defending world champions, the Springboks, were part of the tour. Biggar's wisdom and expertise were invaluable as the team dealt with the pandemic's obstacles.

Dan biggar

1. Training and Preparation Biggar threw himself into the demanding training schedule established by head coach Warren Gatland as soon as he joined the team. The talented Lions team concentrated on building chemistry and unity. Biggar's experience and leadership abilities were crucial in creating a supportive environment inside the team. He was instrumental in bringing players from various countries together by planning team activities and conversations.

2. Performances in Test Matches Biggar had a significant role in the South Africa test matches. The Lions relied heavily on his game management, defensive sturdiness, and tactical kicking.

3. Initial Examination Biggar's accuracy as a kicker was tested in the first test in Cape Town. He demonstrated his dependability as a kicker by contributing vital points through conversions and penalties. Biggar's ability to

Dan biggar

manage the game's tempo proved crucial in the hotly-contested Lions lost by a slim margin, and Biggar's fortitude was on display as he urged his teammates to get back together.

4. The Second Examination In the second test, Biggar further cemented his status as a crucial facilitator. He made excellent decisions that directed the Lions' offensive tactics. Despite a strong effort, the Lions lost to the Springboks once more, which put a lot of pressure on them going into the last match.

5. The Third Exam For the Lions, the last test was a game of life or death, and Biggar delivered. As he guided play and motivated his colleagues to give it their all, his leadership on the field became even more evident. His performance demonstrated his capacity to execute well under duress with crucial defensive plays

Dan biggar
and vital kicks. Biggar's efforts were well acknowledged, but the Lions lost the game in the end, ending the series.

10.3 The Experience's Effect

Biggar's time with the British and Irish Lions was about more than just his on-field exploits; it was also about his development as a person and his friendship with other players.

1. Biggar was able to build close relationships with players from opposing countries while on the Lions tour, which helped to dissolve barriers and promote camaraderie among teammates. Players developed enduring bonds and mutual respect as a result of training and competing together.

Dan biggar

2. Learning from Legends: Biggar benefited greatly from the chance to train with and pick the brains of some of rugby's greatest players. His encounters with seasoned athletes and coaches enhanced his knowledge of the game by revealing various tactics and playing styles.

3. National Pride Representing: Biggar was deeply infused with a sense of pride by the British and Irish Lions. It was a dream come true to be able to compete at such a high level and wear the iconic red jersey, confirming his place among rugby's top players.

10.4 The Lions' Legacy Experience

Even though the Lions may not have been pleased with the series outcome, Dan Biggar's performances on the tour further cemented his status as a premier fly-half. A noteworthy chapter in his rugby career was added by his

Dan biggar

time with the Lions, which demonstrated his skill, leadership, and fortitude in the face of difficulty.

His playing style and mentoring style will surely be influenced by the friendships and lessons he made during the British and Irish Lions tour as he continues his rugby career. In addition to strengthening his legacy as a player, the tour increased his admiration for rugby, the team spirit it promotes, and the players' mutual passion for the game.

Dan biggar

CHAPTER 11: THE BIGGAR KICK ART AND PRECISION

Dan Biggar is well known for his remarkable kicking skills, which blend mental toughness, tactical awareness, and technical brilliance. His kicking technique has developed over years of practice and experience, making it more than just a mechanical procedure. Biggar's ability to kick has become a key component of his style of play, frequently converting games in his team's favor and establishing him as one of rugby's best fly-halves.

11.1 Biggar's Kicking Technical Aspects

Dan biggar

1. Technique for Kicking Biggar's kicking style is distinguished by a smooth action that optimizes accuracy and force. His strategy consists of:

Positioning of the Ball Biggar makes sure the ball is in the best possible position for a clean hit by carefully positioning it on the ground or the tee.

Position of the Body Throughout the kick, he keeps his stance athletic, which permits balance and control. His foot creates the required lift and distance by striking the ball at the sweet spot.

2. For accuracy, Biggar's follow-through is essential. He makes sure the ball follows the desired trajectory by emphasizing a straight follow-through with his kicking leg. His great success percentage with penalties and conversions is a result of his technique's steadiness.

Dan biggar

3. Kick Range Biggar can adjust to many game scenarios thanks to his varied kicking repertoire. Among his range are:

Kicking in Place Biggar is a dependable scorer for his sides because of his reputation for precision under duress and his ability to convert penalties and tries.

Kicking Tactically His ability to perform tactical kicks, including cross-field or grubber kicks, demonstrates his vision and game knowledge. He frequently takes advantage of space and creates scoring opportunities with these kicks.

11.2 Understanding Tactical Situations

1. Reading the Game: Biggar's tactical knowledge is the foundation of his success as a kicker. He has a deep

Dan biggar comprehension of the game, which enables him to spot holes and predict defensive moves. His kicking decisions, whether to go for posts or to find touch, are influenced by this understanding.

2. Management of Games Biggar is essential to game control as a fly-half. He deliberately employs his kicking technique to exert pressure on opposing teams, gain territory, and manage the game's tempo. His leadership and game intelligence are demonstrated by his ability to kick at the ideal time, whether it be for territory or points.

3. Stressful Circumstances Biggar performs exceptionally well under pressure and shows great poise when making kicks at pivotal times. He is a go-to player in close games because of his mental toughness, which enables him to tune out outside distractions and concentrate on the task at hand.

Dan biggar

11.3 Mental Sturdiness

1. Confidence: A major factor in Biggar's success is his faith in his kicking prowess. He has faith in his preparation and technique, and he approaches every kick with optimism. His performance reflects this confidence, which enables him to function well under duress.

2. Routine and Preparation: Biggar stresses the value of planning his kicking technique. He spends time honing his technique so that he is prepared for a variety of kicking situations. His pre-kick routine, which consists of mental repetition and visualization, aids in his ability to stay focused during games.

3. Resilience: Biggar's resilience enables him to recover from missed kicks, which can happen in rugby. He keeps

Dan biggar a growth mindset and views all failures as teaching moments. His ability to remain mentally strong is essential to sustaining his level of performance during a game or competition.

11.4 Effect on the Game

Both at the club and international levels, Biggar's kicking prowess has greatly benefited his sides. His talents go beyond just scoring goals; his kicks frequently alter the course of games and give him significant territorial advantages.

1. Setting an Example: His skill at kicking motivates teammates and fosters an excellence-oriented culture inside the team. Young players frequently admire his technique and poise, picking up important skills from his kicking style.

Dan biggar

2. Strategic Advantage: Biggar's strategic kicking gives his team's style of play a crucial element. His ability to spot openings and take advantage of defensive lapses gives his teammates chances, which frequently result in tries and big scoring opportunities.

3. Game-Changing Moments: Biggar's kicking has changed the course of many games over his career. His ability to kick is still a key component of his game, whether it's a last-minute penalty to win a game or a skillfully performed tactical kick that results in a try.

In conclusion

Dan Biggar's ability to kick is a perfect example of the skill and accuracy needed to be a successful fly-half. His combination of technical proficiency, tactical knowledge, and mental toughness results in a kicking game that is

Dan biggar
both powerful and motivational. Biggar's skill at kicking will continue to be a crucial part of his contributions to rugby throughout his career, inspiring upcoming players and cementing his place among the game's greatest players.

Dan biggar

CHAPTER 12: OFF THE FIELD LIFE FAMILY AND BALANCE

For players like Dan Biggar, striking a balance between the demands of professional athletics and personal life is essential. In his off-field life, Biggar, who is well-known for his rugby skills, places a high value on his family, hobbies, and involvement in the community. This all-encompassing strategy enhances his general well-being in addition to helping him succeed as an athlete.

12.1 Domestic Life

1. Solid Family Foundations: Biggar's family is the center of his life away from the pitch. He values the time

Dan biggar
he spends with his wife and kids and is a devoted father. Amid his rigorous profession, he finds emotional support and stability from family outings, holidays, and everyday moments.

2. Quality Time: Biggar places a high value on spending time with his family and frequently incorporates them into his everyday activities. These occasions, whether they be spent dining together, going to events, or engaging in outdoor pursuits, strengthen family ties and offer a break from the demands of professional rugby.

3. Nurturing Relationships: By devoting time and energy to his family, Biggar creates a supportive atmosphere that enhances his athletic performance and overall well-being. His loved ones' encouragement and support are crucial as he makes his way through the highs and lows of his rugby career.

Dan biggar

12.2 Individual Passions

1. Pursuing Hobbies: Biggar enjoys a variety of pastimes that help him unwind and feel happy when he's not playing. He can relax and refuel by participating in outdoor activities, listening to music, or watching other sports, all of which support a healthy lifestyle.

2. Community Involvement: Biggar uses his position to give back by actively participating in community projects. He stresses the value of helping others and having a positive influence, whether he is coaching young rugby teams or taking part in charitable activities. He finds personal fulfillment and a connection to his heritage through this communal involvement.

3. health activities: Biggar integrates several health activities into his daily routine because he recognizes the significance of both physical and mental well-being. He

Dan biggar places a high priority on his general health to improve performance and personal fulfillment, from mindfulness exercises like meditation to fitness training that supports his rugby work.

12.3 Handling Rugby Obligations

1. Structured Routine: A professional athlete's demanding schedule necessitates proper preparation. Biggar keeps a regimented schedule that makes time for his hobbies, family, and training. He can maximize his productivity and make sure that every area of his life gets the attention it needs because of this arrangement.

2. Open Communication: When it comes to his rugby responsibilities, Biggar favors keeping the lines of communication open with his family. Talking about his schedule makes his loved ones feel connected and

Dan biggar supportive of his profession by fostering understanding and managing expectations in the home.

3. Establishing Boundaries: Biggar consciously attempts to establish boundaries between his personal and professional lives to preserve a positive work-life balance. To completely interact with his loved ones and enjoy life outside of rugby, he makes an effort to disconnect from rugby-related obligations during family time.

12.4 Priorities for the Family

1. Family Time: Biggar values his family greatly and frequently spends time with his wife and kids. He cherishes these times, whether they are spent with his family, on vacation, or just lounging around the house. He understands how important they are for sustaining his

Dan biggar
emotions and keeping him grounded amidst the demands of professional sports.

2. Establishing Stability: Biggar gives his kids a secure and caring environment by emphasizing family life. In addition to improving his family's well-being, this stability gives him the clarity and focus he needs to pursue his rugby career knowing that his loved ones are taken care of.

3. Shared Experiences: Biggar makes enduring memories and fortifies family ties by participating in sports, outdoor excursions, and cultural events with his family. He can refuel away from the rigors of rugby thanks to this time spent together, which creates a loving and supportive environment.

Dan biggar

4. Community Engagement: Biggar is renowned for his participation in neighborhood projects. He spends time giving back to the community, whether it is through youth coaching, local charity events, or encouraging youth athletics. In addition to keeping him rooted in his heritage, this involvement serves as a reminder of the value of cooperation and support in both life and sports.

5. Physical and Mental Health: Biggar places a high priority on his physical and mental well-being to equilibrium. To improve his well-being, he includes fitness practices like yoga and meditation that go beyond rugby training. His emphasis on holistic health fosters resilience and mental clarity while enabling him to handle the physical demands of his job.

In conclusion

Dan biggar

Dan Biggar's principles and priorities are demonstrated by his ability to maintain a healthy balance in his life off the field. In addition to his professional rugby career, he has developed a well-rounded lifestyle by prioritizing his family, enjoying hobbies, and being involved in the community. This equilibrium not only improves his on-field performance but also adds to his general sense of contentment and happiness. Biggar's dedication to upholding this balance will continue to be a defining feature of his career as he negotiates the difficulties of professional athletics.

Dan biggar

CHAPTER 13: SETBACKS AND COMEBACKS

Throughout his career, Welsh rugby union fly-half Dan Biggar has had several noteworthy setbacks and comebacks, demonstrating his tenacity and commitment to the game.

13.1 Failures

1. Early International Difficulties: Biggar first had trouble earning a spot in the Welsh national squad. He had times when he wasn't Wales' first choice and battled to get consistent starts against more gifted fly-halves like Rhys Priestland and James Hook.

Dan biggar

2. 2011 World Cup Exclusion: Biggar did not make the 2011 Rugby World Cup squad, despite demonstrating promise. His early career was severely hampered by this, which motivated him to put in more effort to establish himself on a global scale.

3. Injuries: Biggar has experienced injuries that have limited his playing time and impacted his performance, just like many other rugby players. For instance, injuries restricted his playing time at Northampton Saints, which hindered his ability to establish a steady form.

4. Criticism of Playing Style: Known for his intense and sometimes confrontational playing approach, Biggar has faced criticism over aspects of his game, such as his body language and decision-making under pressure. This scrutiny has occasionally affected his reputation among fans and analysts.

Dan biggar

13.2 Returns

1. 2013 Six Nations Triumph: Biggar made his breakthrough by securing his place as a starting fly-half in the 2013 Six Nations Championship. He began to establish himself as a staple in the national team that year when his performances helped Wales win the Six Nations title.

2. 2015 Rugby World Cup: Biggar put up impressive performances during the 2015 World Cup, notably a stunning performance against England at Twickenham where he scored 23 points and guided Wales to a thrilling victory. His reputation as a top fly-half was cemented by this.

Dan biggar

3. British & Irish Lions trips: Biggar's skill and tenacity won him selection for the British & Irish Lions trips in 2017 and 2021. Making the squad was a major accomplishment and a high point in his career, even though injuries and competition limited his appearances.

4. Leadership and Captaincy: Due to injuries to several senior players, Biggar was named captain of the Welsh Six Nations team in 2022. Wales encountered difficulties under his leadership, but they persevered and fought back, demonstrating his development as a capable leader both on and off the field.

In summary, Dan Biggar's career was characterized by early setbacks and critiques that forced him to grow and change. He has overcome scrutiny, injuries, and rivalry to establish a reputation for his leadership, tactical skill, and passionate style of play. He has a strong mental

Dan biggar toughness and a strong desire to represent his teams at the greatest level, as evidenced by his comebacks.

Dan biggar

CHAPTER 14: THE BIGGAR'S LEGACY AND THE NEXT GENERATION

Dan Biggar's career in rugby is defined by his fierce enthusiasm, astute tactical judgment, and capacity to stand up when things count. An outline of his legacy and his impact on the following generation may be found here:

14.1 The Legacy of Biggar

1. Consistency and Reliability: Biggar has been a reliable member of Wales' squad as well as the clubs he

Dan biggar has represented, including the Northampton Saints and the Ospreys. He has established himself as a mainstay in the side with his accurate goal-kicking, tactical game management, and defensive perseverance, particularly in important international competitions like the Six Nations and Rugby World Cups.

2. Clutch Performer: Biggar's reputation as a clutch player has been cemented by his capacity to perform well under duress. Welsh rugby history will never be the same after memorable events like his game-winning drop goals and high-pressure penalty kicks.

3. Defensive Commitment: Biggar has distinguished himself with his physicality and defensive prowess, in contrast to many fly-halves who are mostly recognized for their offensive performance. Younger players are encouraged to take a more well-rounded approach by his

Dan biggar dedication to tackling and contesting high balls, which has established a benchmark for his position.

4. Leadership: His 2022 Six Nations leadership demonstrated his development from a fierce competitor into a capable leader who could motivate and inspire his players. He went from being a dependable player to a leader in Welsh rugby as a result of this job.

14.2 Impact on the Upcoming Generation

1. Mentorship: Younger players on both club and national teams look up to Biggar because of his professionalism and expertise. Prospective fly-halves

Dan biggar and backs try to imitate his work ethic, tactical acumen, and fortitude.

2. Technical Mastery: From his trademark Biggar Shuffle before goal-kicking to his strategic high-ball game, Biggar's emphasis on technical accuracy has impacted the younger generation. His strategies have been imitated by players to improve their own mental toughness and consistency.

3. Increasing Standards: Biggar's emphasis on meticulousness and high standards has reverberated, encouraging a culture of excellence among up-and-coming Welsh talent. The standard that Biggar set has forced players like Gareth Anscombe, Callum Sheedy, and up-and-coming fly-halves to improve.

Dan biggar

4. Global Impact: His time with the British & Irish Lions and Northampton Saints has also demonstrated to future players that Welsh rugby talent can succeed on a larger scale. Others have been inspired to strive for both club and international success as a result of this.

14.3 Prospects for the Future

Wales looks to players like Anscombe, Sheedy, and up-and-coming players like Sam Costelow to take over as Biggar's international career comes to an end. These players, who grew up in a rugby culture that was shaped by Biggar's example, seek to combine their special qualities with his tactical acumen and spirit of battle.

Dan Biggar's legacy is rooted in both his accomplishments and the motivation he offers the following generation. He has established a standard for

Dan biggar
how a fly-half can be resilient, astute, and a successful team leader.

Dan biggar

CHAPTER 15: LOOKING FORWARD BEYOND THE PITCH

Dan Biggar has a nuseveralortunities to make a big impression as he moves into the next stage of his career, away from the rugby field:

15.1 Mentoring and Coaching

Biggar's extensive knowledge of the game would make coaching an obvious next step. He is well-positioned to coach up-and-coming players because of his strategic approach and first-hand knowledge gained as a fly-half and captain. He might be able to coach club teams or

Dan biggar perhaps the Welsh Rugby Union, helping to shape the next generation of backline and fly-halves.

15.2 Analysis and Punditry

Biggar's frank and fervent personality would work well in sports media. Many former rugby players have made a smooth transition into analyst and commentator positions, providing commentary during live matches and helping with pre- and post-match research. He would be a respected voice in rugby conversations, offering in-depth analyses and judgments due to his expertise and tactical knowledge.

15.3 Supporting the Welfare of Players

Dan biggar

Biggar may act as an advocate for player welfare because he has personally experienced the physical strain and pains of playing rugby at the highest level. He might utilize his position to advocate for athletes' well-being, concentrating on topics like injury prevention, mental health support, and career transition aid, whether he is collaborating with player associations or leading campaigns for improved health and safety regulations in the sport.

15.4 Ambassadership for Rugby

By taking part in initiatives to expand rugby in areas where it is still in its infancy, Biggar's profile might be used to promote rugby internationally. He may motivate future players and spread rugby principles through coaching clinics, collaborations with rugby federations,

Dan biggar or ambassadorial positions with global rugby organizations.

15.5 Volunteering and Community Service

Dan Biggar could assist causes that are important to him by using his platform for charitable endeavors. He might support social projects in Wales or throughout the world that concentrate on youth development, sports access, or educational efforts by starting his foundation or working with already-existing charities.

15.6 Entrepreneurship

Dan biggar

Biggar, like many athletes, may look into business ventures that fit with his hobbies. This could involve investing in more general business endeavors or starting sports-related businesses like training academies or collaborations with sporting brands.

In brief

Beyond rugby, Dan Biggar appears to have a bright career ahead of him, full of chances to use his skills, charisma, and leadership. His possible post-playing career path of coaching, journalism, activism, or business guarantees that his influence will endure both inside and outside of the rugby community.

Dan biggar

CHAPTER 16: REFLECTION FROM A RUGBY LEGEND

Themes of tenacity, passion, and thankfulness would probably be at the forefront of Dan Biggar's thoughts if he were to look back on his career as a rugby legend. His reflections could sound like this:

1. Perseverance: Through Difficulties Biggar would likely discuss the difficulties he encountered in his early career, such as battling for a starting spot in the Welsh squad and recuperating from injuries. He can consider how such difficulties helped him become a more resilient player by instilling in him the value of perseverance and mental toughness. His tale is one of overcoming

Dan biggar skepticism and criticism to become more driven to succeed.

16.1 Taking Pride in Wales' Representation

Biggar would probably express great delight in representing his country at the greatest level, as wearing the Welsh jersey has always meant everything to him. He would talk about the thrilling environment of playing in the Six Nations, the team spirit in the locker room, and the excitement of times when he helped the team win and boost morale.

16.2 Characteristics

Biggar's thoughts may bring to light some of his career's high points, like his outstanding performance against

Dan biggar
England in the 2015 Rugby World Cup or his crucial contribution to the Six Nations victories. In addition to defining his career, these occasions gave teammates and supporters alike unforgettable happy memories. He would consider the importance of such triumphs and their meaning for him.

16.3 Leadership Lessons Learned

Biggar would probably consider how such experiences helped him to be more than just a player after assuming leadership duties, such as captaining the Welsh team. He might talk about how being a leader changed him, enabling him to strike a balance between his enthusiasm and his cool, and how mentoring younger players was just as rewarding as reaching personal goals.

Dan biggar

16.4 Appreciation of Mentors and Supporters

Biggar's thoughts would probably include sincere appreciation for the mentors, teammates, and supporters who helped him along the way. Important areas of reflection would be recognizing his family's efforts and the guidance he received from coaches and seasoned athletes who shaped his path.

16.5 Establishing a Heritage

When Biggar considers his legacy, he may express his wish that he has motivated the upcoming generation to play with passion and tenacity. Whether he won or lost, he would like to be known as a player who always gave it his all on the field. He wants young athletes to

Dan biggar understand that a great competitor plays with pride and perseverance.

16.6 Toward the Future

Biggar would conclude by considering the future, not only for himself but also for Welsh rugby and the game in general. He would say that he wanted to keep making a difference, whether it was by advocating, coaching, or mentoring so that his love of rugby would continue in fresh and significant ways.

These observations would tell the tale of a guy who devoted his life to the sport, saw every failure as a teaching moment, and had a lasting impression on people around him, in addition to that of a celebrated athlete.

Dan biggar

CONCLUSION

To sum up, Dan Biggar's transformation from a driven teenage athlete to a revered rugby hero is a prime example of the qualities of tenacity, passion, and leadership. He overcame early setbacks, injuries, and criticism to forge a career filled with crucial plays and clutch situations that improved his team's performance and reputation. His pride in representing Wales, his tactical skill on the field, and his unwavering dedication to perfection are the foundations of his legacy.

Biggar's impact is felt off the field as well because he mentors younger players and exemplifies perseverance. His perspective positions in coaching, commentary, and advocacy promise to further his beneficial influence on the rugby community as he adjusts to life after playing.

Dan biggar

Biggar's narrative demonstrates how commitment and Heart have the power to inspire future generations and turn failures into victories.

The lasting impact Dan Biggar had on Welsh rugby and the example he set for aspiring sportsmen will be more significant than the number of games he won.

www.ingramcontent.com/pod-product-compliance
Lightning Source LLC
Chambersburg PA
CBHW071033240526
45469CB00006BD/2194